"This little book is about parenting [illegible] *p not parenting as a* [illegible] *our children a* [illegible] *fore a proper vi*[illegible]*."*

Dr. E[illegible] [illegible]d
Discipleshi[illegible]sonville;
Fello[illegible], Certified Conciliator, The
Institute for Christian Conciliation

"I can't think of a pastor or biblical counselor I trust more to speak on this topic. As a father of five myself, I trust Paul's insights and his practical application of Scripture to parenting. This is a must-read for parents! My wife and I just devoured it!"

Josh Weidmann, author and
Senior Pastor, Grace Chapel, Englewood

"In a 'me' culture, this book helps us draw the inward gaze of our children upward to our amazing God. It is the right balance of challenging and hopeful, theological and practical. As a pastor and father of four, I will be using it and giving it to those I know."

Kim Kira, Teaching Elder, Lighthouse
Community Church, Torrance

"This book is bravely countercultural. In a world which instructs children to 'search for the hero inside themselves,' we can be tempted to downplay God's holiness and our own need for salvation. This book will help you redirect your family's gaze upwards to a truly awesome God who is to be feared, adored, and obeyed. With many practical applications, it will encourage you to trust God's life-giving word to shape in your children's hearts a biblical and liberating self-image."

Sally Gobbett, pastor's wife and mum of four

"I highly recommend Raising Kids in a 'You Can Do It' World *to all parents who seek to raise Christ-centered kids in a self-centered world. Tautges lays a solid biblical foundation for how we are to view God and ourselves. He gives practical step-by-step guidance for meaningful conversations with our kids. He reminds us, 'We are not good parents attempting to raise good children; we are sinners saved by grace who are depending upon God, and pleading with Him, to graciously give eternal life to our children, through the gospel, by means of His grace.'"*

Sara Wallace, author of *The Gospel-Centered Mom* and *For the Love of Discipline*

RAISING KIDS

in a "You Can Do It!" World

Also in this series:

Raising Kids in a Screen-Saturated World
Raising Kids in the Way of Grace
Raising Teens in a Hyper-Sexualized World

RAISING KIDS

in a "You Can Do It!" World

Help for Parents

Paul Tautges

10 Publishing
a division of 10 of those.com

First published in Great Britain in 2018

British Library Cataloguing in Publication Data
A record for this book is available from the British Library

ISBN: 978-1-912373-46-8

Designed by Pete Barnsley (CreativeHoot.com)
Printed in Denmark by Nørhaven

10Publishing, a division of 10ofthose.com
Unit C, Tomlinson Road, Leyland, PR25 2DY, England

Email: info@10ofthose.com
Website: www.10ofthose.com

CONTENTS

SERIES INTRODUCTION

Raising kids is a daunting endeavor for even the most skilled parents. The challenge is compounded by the high-tempo lives we live. Between work, school, practices, recitals, games, youth group, performances, time with friends, and the myriad of other time-suckers, parenting feels more like a logistical nightmare than the divine call to shape the lives of our children.

We have partnered with 10Publishing to produce the *Raising Kids* series. These resources have been written to bring welcome help to parents who may be feeling overwhelmed by the many challenges parenting brings. The series contains short books on vital issues parents face in today's day and age, as well as issues parents of every generation wrestle with. Issues like a self-made identity, sex, gender fluidity, our results-driven culture, grace-centered parenting, technology, and social media, are all covered in these books. The authors write from a deep understanding of God's Word coupled with their own experience of raising kids, making each book rich with practical and personal wisdom that is sure to benefit any parent.

These short, easy-to-read books do not attempt to be exhaustive manuals on any one of the topics. Instead, they offer strategic insights that are both timeless and immediately applicable. The goal is not to fully outfit you for an expedition over Everest but to give you a few secure handholds and footholds that will help you hang on and advance up the mountain of raising kids.

Our children are being taught at school that they are awesome and that they can achieve anything they want if only they try hard enough. This message can seem at odds with what the Bible teaches, and the cultural tension can be confusing for our kids. *In Raising Kids in a "You Can Do It" World*, Paul Tautges explains how we can help our children see how awesome God is which in turn will help them to have a biblical self-image that leads to true and lasting humble confidence.

Curtis W. Solomon
Director, The Biblical Counseling Coalition

IS EVERYONE AWESOME?

From almost every angle (movies, TV, YouTube, school) our kids are receiving the same basic message. They hear that every child is his or her own independent, self-sufficient, self-directed, self-governing person. Like a scratched vinyl record, the world expresses related mantras:

- You're awesome!
- Be who you are on the inside.
- Listen to your heart.
- You can do it!

Instead of helping kids to become confident, stable, and secure—because of humble dependency upon God and His wisdom—

messages like these feed the inborn, natural elevation of self. Awareness of this cultural tension highlights how much we need to approach Christian parenting as intentional discipleship. Like every parent, every child is a depraved sinner whose heart naturally gravitates toward personal autonomy. Therefore (also like their parents), every kid's greatest need is to be redeemed by the grace of God, and renewed according to the image of Jesus Christ.

So how can we help our kids think rightly about themselves and God? How can we train them to see themselves as God's special creatures, while at the same time not lead them to believe they are the masters of their own destiny?

The purpose of this book is to answer these kinds of questions. To simplify matters for you (not that the answer or the application is simple!) I will draw a basic road map for parenting in today's world, with eight road signs marking the landmark truths our kids need to understand. I will assume that you, the parent, are driving (or at least you want to) the car that carries your kids down this road. I trust that you want to say to them, "Listen, my son, to your father's instruction and do not forsake your mother's teaching" (Prov. 1:8).

Therefore, I want to come alongside you to provide you with biblical guidance. This book is not aimed at your kids; it's aimed at you, it's aimed at me. That being said, however, at the end of the book you will find age-appropriate questions to help you discuss the truths you learn with your children.

What are the most important signs to read and follow? Fasten your seatbelt. Here we go.

SIGNPOST 1

TEST YOUR OWN FAITH

To lead our children toward a God-centered view of life, we must begin at the beginning. That is, before we get too gung-ho about directing our children to follow Jesus, we should take careful inventory of our own relationship with God.

Are you saved? Have you experienced conversion? Are you seriously following Jesus as a committed disciple? Are you growing in the grace and knowledge of Christ, or are you content to possess superficial faith? Are you moving away from loving the world, or are you tiptoeing as close to the edge as you can?

In other words, what *you as a parent* believe about God, sin, and salvation—the gospel—

and how you live out these beliefs day by day impacts your children.

Beware of three common errors

When it comes to teaching children the gospel, there are mistakes which are often made by Christian parents. I'll mention three.

1. Fatalism

Some parents become so enamored by the beauty of God's sovereignty in salvation (and we *should* be enamored by His sovereign grace!) that they take a hands-off approach to evangelizing their children. "After all," they might think, "if God plans to save my kids, then He will do it with or without me." However, the biblical view of God's sovereign grace never minimizes our responsibility to obey the gospel or share it with others. Therefore, what every child really needs is regular instruction from Scripture concerning God's holy character, man's sinful nature, and God's provision for salvation through Jesus Christ. This instruction will naturally lead to conversations in which we may gently help our children to see their own need for the Savior, and call them to personal faith. For example, the apostle Paul writes how Timothy had "known the Holy Scriptures" from infancy because of the faithful instruction of his mother and grandmother. As a result, the Spirit used Scripture to make him "wise for salvation through faith in Christ Jesus" (2 Tim. 1:5; 3:15).

2. "Easy Decisionism"

In a sincere effort to make the gospel easy to understand, and heaven easy to attain, parents may unknowingly offer salvation as a low-priced transaction between a sinner and God: "You don't want to go to hell when you die, do you? Then just pray this simple prayer." Or, "Do you want to go to heaven someday? Just ask Jesus into your heart." However, what every child really needs is to be regularly confronted by two costs: (1) the cost God paid to make salvation free for sinners, and (2) the cost of discipleship. First, remember that salvation is free for us, but it was not free for God! The price was the blood of His only Son (1 Pet. 1:19). But second, let's also teach our children that the call of Jesus to enter the kingdom of God requires walking through the narrow gate that "leads to life, and only a few find it" (Matt. 7:14). Of course we also need to be praying that God would work in our children's hearts to bring them to repentance and faith even as we faithfully teach them the gospel.

3. False Assurance

Some Christian parents, disillusioned by their child's rebellion, worldliness, or plain lack of interest in spiritual things, fail to directly confront them with biblical truth. Instead, they assure their carnal child he or she is saved when the Bible indicates there is a possibility they're not. Perhaps they reason, regardless of their child's carnality, "I just know my son is saved because I was with him when he knelt by his bed and prayed to receive Jesus." However, what every child really needs is to be gently guided in the use of Scripture to see their own sinfulness, learn how to examine their own rebellious heart, and evaluate the presence or absence of the fruit of the Spirit in order to see if they have been deceived. James 1:22 warns believers, "Do not merely listen to the word, and so deceive yourselves." Christian parents must be careful not to unintentionally feed their child's self-deception by giving them false assurance. Remember, even Jesus had a Judas.

Now, I don't say this to cast doubt upon the genuineness of your faith. I don't even know you! However, I do mean to make it clear that it's hypocritical for us as parents to expect our children to go further with *their* faith than we are willing to go with *ours*. So let's be honest and humble. Let's regularly examine our own lives before the mirror of the Word of God so that we do not forget the depth of our own need for Christ and His saving grace (Jas. 1:21–25).

Take a moment to reflect

In 1 Corinthians 11:27–28, the apostle Paul admonishes us to examine ourselves each time we gather to "eat of the bread and drink from the cup," so that we do not partake in an "unworthy manner" and "be guilty of sinning against the body and blood of the Lord". If Jesus instituted communion as an ordinance to be practiced regularly, and the apostle urges us to examine ourselves every time we partake, then surely the spiritual discipline of self-examination is reasonable and should be an ongoing practice in the Christian life. Therefore, let us also heed the apostle's later admonition: "Examine yourselves to see whether you are in the faith; test yourselves" (2 Cor. 13:5).

Take some time right now to prayerfully evaluate your own spiritual life. Are you just as eager for God to teach you to walk in the obedience of faith as you are to guide your children?

SIGNPOST 2

TREASURE GOD AND HIS WORD

A significant marker on the road to raising kids to walk humbly with God is the integration of the Word of God into every area of life. This is necessary if our kids are to grow in the fear of the Lord, which will be defined in the next chapter. Right now, I urge you to think about the place Scripture currently occupies in your own heart and home. This is a high priority because our children's devotion to the Bible is influenced by our own treasuring of Scripture, or the lack of it.

The virtues of Scripture are endless, for sure. But let me draw your attention to three reasons we should turn our heart's affection toward the Bible.

The Bible is God's trustworthy word

We and our children need to embrace the Bible as the infallible self-disclosure of God through which He reveals Himself to us. Through creation, God has revealed His power and majesty for all to see (Ps. 19:1–6; Rom. 1:20). But it is only through the message of Scripture, crystallized in the gospel, that we come to experience the transforming power of God's redemptive grace, in relationship with Him, through Christ (Ps. 19:7–12; John 15:4–5). For this relationship to prosper, we need to grow in knowing God better—His majesty, glory, mercy, love, and sovereignty (among others). Knowing God, and how He is intimately acquainted with us, stabilizes our souls. As the Holy Spirit uses Scripture to draw us into a closer relationship with God, we in turn become more accurate reflectors of His glory. This explains why Jesus prayed for His disciples in the past, and prays for us now, "Sanctify them by the truth; your word is truth" (John 17:17).

The Bible is our necessary bread

Scripture is not only God's trustworthy message to man, but it is the soul-satisfying food in which we should delight (Ps. 119:16, 77). As we grow in treasuring the Word of God, we gradually come to realize that our souls cannot thrive without it, and our resolve to stand strong in the face of temptation strengthens. When Satan tempted Jesus to selfishly turn stones into bread to remedy His own hunger, Jesus answered, "It is written: 'Man shall not live on bread alone, but on every word that comes from the mouth of God'" (Matt. 4:4). And the prophet Jeremiah testified, "When your words came, I ate them; they were my joy and my heart's delight" (Jer. 15:16).

Whether it's the latest video game or smart phone, the "hottest" styles in clothing, or the latest movie trailer, our kids' world is filled with things which bring a certain amount of pleasure. But the pleasure won't last. As parents, we know it won't because we used to think the same way. What a gift we give to our children when, through example and prayer, we watch their appetite for the Word of God grow!

The Bible is a mirror revealing our true self

Scripture is a penetrating mirror reflecting the true condition of our soul. Every morning (I hope!) we all look into a wall mirror to make sure we are at least presentable to the rest of the human race. But as much as we all would love to own a mirror that always makes us look good, mirrors don't lie. They bring us good news and bad news; they give proof that we may have lost or gained a few pounds, or they reveal one more wrinkle creeping away from our eye. Scripture does the same thing; it reveals the amazing grace of God toward sinners, while also identifying what heart complications remain in us as God's saints. It tells it like it is; it reveals our true self, as James teaches us:

> *Do not merely listen to the word, and so deceive yourselves. Do what it says. Anyone who listens to the word but does not do what it says is like someone who looks at his face in a mirror and, after looking at himself, goes away and immediately forgets what he looks like (Jas. 1:22–24).*

God never intended us to read or study the Bible for intellectual benefit alone. Instead, He breathed it out of His mind so that we may know Him, so that our hearts would be born anew and our lives progressively transformed into the image of His Son. As our children learn to embrace the unchanging Word of God, their minds are prepared to evaluate the fluid teachings of men, hold dear to truth, and reject the ideas which do not fit within its divinely inspired framework.

Take a moment to pray

As parents, we need to set an example of being hungry for God. The apostle Peter exhorts us to be like newborn babies who "crave pure spiritual milk, so that by it you may grow up in your salvation" (1 Pet. 2:2). Our own growth in Christ directly hinges upon our appetite for the Word. If this chapter has challenged your heart, and you recognize that your own hunger for the Bible is not what it should be, spend a few minutes in prayer. Confess your lack of spiritual appetite to God, and ask for His forgiveness. Then ask Him to give you a hunger and thirst for the Word which will become contagious in your home.

SIGNPOST 3

TRAIN THEM TO FEAR THE LORD

The "fear of the Lord" is a phrase that was once common among Christians, but has lost favor in recent decades. Nevertheless, it's a necessary component in the nurture and admonition of our children. To say it another way, it's an essential part of the "spiritual curriculum" we should teach our children, a heart virtue we should pray for and labor to instill.

Proverbs 9:10 teaches, "The fear of the LORD is the beginning of wisdom, and knowledge of the Holy One is understanding." Commenting on this verse, R. C. Sproul writes, "The focus here is on a sense of awe and respect for the majesty of God."[1] Fundamentally, then, what it means to fear the Lord is to be in such awe of Him that it produces a desire to worship and obey Him by living within His authority structures (home, church, school, government, employment). If we want our children to function well in this world then, without question, we should want them to fear the Lord!

Heart attitude is the key

The fear of the Lord begins in the heart, with our attitude. Like every other attitude, it works itself out in how we live and love. In other words, when the attitude of our heart is one of reverence before God, then we will desire to live in a way that brings Him glory. The same is true for our kids. Since the Bible consistently argues that all behavior flows from the heart, we must see our role as spiritual shepherds of the hearts of our children. In his foundation-building book *Shepherding a Child's Heart*, Tedd Tripp hits the nail on the head when he exhorts us to keep our eyes on our children's hearts as we parent:

> *The central focus of parenting is the gospel. You need to direct not simply the behavior of your children, but the attitudes of their hearts. You need to show them not just the "what" of their sin and failure, but the "why." Your children desperately need to understand not only the external "what" they did wrong, but also the internal "why" they did it. You must help them see that God works from the inside out. Therefore, your parenting goal cannot simply be well behaved children. Your children must also understand why they sin and how to recognize internal change.*[2]

As parents, we have a stewardship from God. We have been entrusted with immortal souls who will live for eternity in one of two places: heaven or hell. Therefore, our longing should be to nurture our kids in such a way that the soil of their hearts may be prepared to receive the seed of the gospel which alone leads to eternal life.

To fear the Lord is to be in awe of Him

In the following verses, notice how fear and awe are connected:

> *Let all the earth fear the LORD; let all the inhabitants of the world stand in awe of him! (Ps. 33:8; ESV).*

> *My flesh trembles in fear of you; I stand in awe of your laws (Ps. 119:120).*

This connection is maintained in the New Testament, even after the work of Christ makes it possible for us to be reconciled to the holy God:

> *Therefore, since we are receiving a kingdom that cannot be shaken, let us be thankful, and so worship God acceptably with reverence and awe, for our "God is a consuming fire." (Heb. 12:28–29).*

The work of Jesus on the cross appeased God's wrath against our sin. Therefore, we may now reverently approach God through faith in Jesus Christ. The blood of the Lamb of God was shed so that we may be drawn back into a loving relationship with our Maker. In Christ, our Creator becomes our Father.

Protect the marriage of punishment and mercy

How is it possible for unrighteous sinners like us to be at peace with the holy God? It's only possible if the one who is perfectly righteous—God—is also the one who provides the path to peace with Him. Again, this is made possible only because of the cross of Jesus.

At Calvary, divine love and faithfulness met together, righteousness and peace kissed each other (Ps. 85:10). Because the Son of God willingly offered Himself as the perfect substitute to be punished in our place, and God the angry Judge accepted the Son's sacrifice, the righteous demand was met at the same time that indescribable love was displayed. Keeping this gospel truth central is the only way we can have joy in fearing God, as Jerry Bridges explains:

> *Had sin never entered the world it still would be fitting for us to fear God—to bow in reverential awe before Him. We would gladly join the seraphs in calling out, "Holy, holy, holy is the Lord Almighty; the whole earth is full of his glory." But sin did enter the*

> *world—and because of His holiness, God now reveals Himself as the hater of sin and the just punisher of sinners. But He also reveals Himself in the person of His Son as a merciful and gracious Savior. Our awe of His holiness can be joined with amazement at His love.*[3]

Only through the gospel may our awe of God's holiness be joined with amazement at His love. Because of Jesus, we may sing "Holy, Holy, Holy, Lord God Almighty"[4] followed immediately by "Amazing Grace, how sweet the sound that saved a wretch like me".[5]

In case you're wondering why I think this is important to say in a parenting book, think it through with me. Salvation comes to those who recognize they need it. If our kids don't have a sense of their own sinfulness, then there will be no logical reason for them to sense their need for the Savior. Training our children in the fear of the Lord will heighten the awareness of their own sinfulness and, consequently, move them toward God's remedy in Jesus Christ. But how can we cultivate the fear of the Lord in their hearts?

Before entering the Promised Land, God told Moses, "Gather the people to me, that I may let them hear my words, so that they may learn to fear me all the days that they live on the earth, and that they may teach their children so" (Deut. 4:10; ESV). Our fear of the Lord is directly related to our attitude toward the Bible. Therefore, as mentioned in the last chapter, we should give priority to the Word. We can do this in a couple of ways. Practicing family Bible reading demonstrates its importance. Applying Scripture's authority to our kids' disobedience (when we apply correction and discipline) establishes its authority as the basis of ours.

Take a moment to reflect

How would you describe your heart's attitude toward the Lord? Toward the Bible? Have you become too casual with God? Have you lost your awe of Him? Pray to Him, "Teach me your way, LORD … give me an undivided heart, that I may fear your name" (Ps. 86:11).

SIGNPOST 4

TEACH THEM GOD IS AWESOME

"Awesome" is one word which has become so commonplace it is at risk of losing its punch. Today, it's used to describe anything from a chef's pizza to an artist's portrait, a baseball team's double play to a restaurant's double cheeseburger. For this reason, day in and day out, it's not unusual for our kids to hear that they and their accomplishments are awesome.

God is awesome

Originally, the word "awesome" referred to "something which inspires awe." Awe is an overwhelming feeling of reverence, admiration, or fear produced by that which is grand, sublime, or extremely powerful. I don't know about you, but I've never met a pizza that fits that description! But "awesome" is a perfect word to describe God and the works He performs:

> *Who among the gods is like you, LORD? Who is like you—majestic in holiness, awesome in glory, working wonders? (Ex. 15:11).*

> *For the LORD Most High is awesome, the great King over all the earth (Ps. 47:2).*

> *Come and see what God has done, his awesome deeds for mankind! (Ps. 66:5).*

Since God is awesome, He's worthy of our lives revolving around Him. Seeing God as awesome naturally leads to adoration, humility, and submission. For example, it was when the prophet Isaiah saw the holy God in His majestic glory that he found his proper place as a worshiper. Once he confessed his sin to God, the prophet was then forgiven and ready to serve God (Is. 6).

As parents, we should ask ourselves if our kids see in us an awe for God. In the way we speak and live, they need to see our reverence for the Lord.

God is the Creator of all

One of the things I love about children is how readily they accept that God is their Creator; they easily believe He made them *by* Himself and *for* Himself (Is. 43:7). This explains why the first sentence in the Bible remains the most foundational truth of all: "In the beginning God created the heavens and the earth" (Gen. 1:1). It's even the reason we have seven days in every week:

> *For in six days the LORD made the heavens and the earth, the sea, and all that is in them, but he rested on the seventh day. Therefore the LORD blessed the Sabbath day and made it holy (Ex. 20:11).*

This simple, introductory truth about God impacts our parenting in more ways than we perhaps realize. When we instill in our children an awe for God as their Creator, we establish the starting point for any sense of accountability. We point them to the only firm anchoring point for living in this fallen, stormy world. We also prepare them to receive biblical warnings like "Remember your Creator in the days of your youth" (Ecc. 12:1), and "God will bring every deed into judgment, including every hidden thing, whether it is good or evil" (Ecc. 12:14).

God is a hard worker

We may have never thought of God as the hardest worker of all, but the Bible opens with God working, creating the heavens and the earth, both seen and unseen. On the sixth day, when He created man in His image, God commanded him to be a worker too. But sin affected our entire world, even the world of work. Weeds took over the ground. Work became more difficult and less enjoyable. However, in Christ, God redeems work. For this reason, He exhorts us to work "with sincerity of heart and reverence for the Lord. Whatever you do, work at it with all your heart, as working for the Lord" (Col. 3:22–23). Here the apostle Paul connects the concept of reverence for the Lord to a hearty work ethic.

When we model hard work accompanied by an honorable attitude toward our employer, we elevate the dignity of work, and demonstrate to our kids how new ownership in Christ impacts every area of life.

These truths matter in parenting, since our kids' view of God will impact whether they grow up to be lazy or diligent workers. God's works testify that He indeed is awesome. As Creator and Redeemer, He is the only One who is always worthy to be loved, obeyed, and worshiped—not just on Sunday, but every day of the week.

Let's get practical

Our kids need us to teach them that God is awesome and His works shout "Glory!" They need us to keep God exalted. Let me give you some examples of how we may do this, practically speaking, just by slightly altering the focus of our praise:

- When our 10-year-old son makes a great play at first base, I could say, "Buddy, you are awesome!" *Or* I could say, "Buddy, that was excellent. Isn't

God awesome to give you the ability to play baseball?"

- When our 12-year-old daughter takes first place in a swim meet, I could say, "Sweetie, you're amazing. Your swimming is awesome!" *Or* I could say, "Sweetie, I am so thankful the Lord designed you to be a great swimmer. Isn't He awesome for doing that?"
- When our 16-year-old son is nominated Employee of the Month, I could say, "You are so awesome!" *Or* I could say, "I'm so proud of you for being an exceptional worker. Your excellent work ethic brings glory to our awesome God."
- When our 21-year-old daughter makes the Dean's List for the third semester in a row, I could say, "Wow! You are an awesome college student." *Or* I could say, "Wow! God continues to bless your diligence. Thank you for working so hard and bringing glory to our awesome God."

Okay, you get the idea. The difference is subtle, I know. But these examples show how being more intentional in our affirmation may prompt a Godward look. Our goal should be to raise not self-confident children, but God-dependent adults.

SIGNPOST 5

THRILL THEM WITH THE GOSPEL

A Christian home can be a dangerous place for a child's soul. There, I said it. But what do I mean? Let me illustrate.

Out of loving concern for their wellbeing, we protect our children from polio and other dangerous diseases by giving them a vaccine. Basically, we ask the doctor to inject a germ (a weakened version of the pathogen) into their body in order to trigger their immune system to build antibodies. This tricks the immune system by creating a false memory of having fought off the disease in the past. That way, if or when they encounter the full-blown virus, their body will say, "No problem. Been there. Done that."

If we're not careful, we may inadvertently do the same thing with the gospel. Let me explain. In our sincere desire to see our children become Christians, we may offer them a weakened strain of the gospel, or speak of salvation in such commonplace fashion that we inoculate them against it. If we have an inordinate desire to see them "make a decision for Christ," we may offer them a watered-down version of the gospel just to get "results." But what happens when they encounter the more complete picture of the gospel, of what their own sin really did to the Son of God? Will they be inoculated against the real thing? Will they carelessly say, "Been there. Done that"?

Additionally, in our effort to protect our children from the damaging influence and painful consequences of sin, we may be tempted to substitute a moralistic gospel for the real thing. Our desire to do a good job raising our kids may tempt us to settle for a message like, "Just be good. Be nice. You can do it." By doing so, we may undermine the convicting work of the Holy Spirit which prepares them for the good news.

However, we can guard against this. I believe one of the best ways is to thrill them with God's gospel of grace. And that begins with us. Your kids, and mine, need parents who have never gotten over the wonders of God's grace toward rebellious sinners. Our kids don't need perfect parents. They need parents who know how desperately they need the Savior themselves. Creating this atmosphere in our homes will inspire many opportunities to talk about the saving work of Christ in normal, everyday conversation.

Four key truths

When thinking and speaking of the good news, always keep the following four truths in mind: God is holy and righteous; we are sinful and rebellious; Jesus is the answer; but we must respond.

1. God is holy and righteous

Understanding the gospel begins with an understanding of God's holy character and righteous demands. If we neglect this foundation, there is no way to point our kids to a standard they cannot meet. And without an established, unattainable standard, there is no need for the good news of the gospel. Be sure to teach your kids that, even though God made us in His image, and loves us, He is too holy to associate with us (Hab. 1:13). Help them to understand God's demand for perfect righteousness (Matt. 5:48), which then leads to a discussion regarding how His justice requires Him to punish all sinners (Rom. 1:18–20).

2. We are sinful and rebellious

In contrast to the holiness of God, be sure to teach your kids the truth about their own spiritual condition as a sinner. The word "gospel" means "good news." However, this good news loses its meaning and significance if an understanding of the bad news is not gained first. This is why it's an evangelistic mistake to immediately jump to "Jesus loves you and has a wonderful plan for your life." The bad news includes at least three fundamental truths: we are born sinful (Ps. 51:5); we prove our sinful nature by our thoughts, words, desires, and actions (Rom. 1–3); and we are prone to wander from God (Is. 53:6). The result is that we are enemies of God who are separated from Him by our sin (Rom. 5:10).

3. Jesus is the answer

But there is good news! Yes, every one of us is a guilty sinner deserving eternal punishment. We are all like sheep who have "gone astray, each of us has turned to our own way," but there is great hope for us since "the LORD has laid on him [Jesus Christ] the iniquity of us all" (Is. 53:6). God gave His one and only Son for us (John 3:16). Jesus is both sinless God and fully man and, therefore, qualified to be the only mediator between God and man (1 Tim. 2:5). As the one mediator, Jesus died *for* sin, in our place, as the only acceptable sacrifice (1 Pet. 3:18), rose from the dead (Rom. 4:25), and is alive today to intercede for those who turn to Him (Heb. 7:25). Jesus is the only Savior (John 14:6; Acts 4:12) and the Lord to be obeyed (Luke 6:46).

4. But we (including our kids) must respond

God's love and mercy have provided the way for us to be saved from the penalty of sin. However, this gift of grace—the gift of righteousness—must be received personally, even by good children being brought up in a good home. The Bible commands us to repent and believe the gospel (Mark 1:15), and Romans 10:9–10 explains this further:

> *If you declare with your mouth, "Jesus is Lord," and believe in your heart that God raised him from the dead, you will be saved. For it is with your heart that you believe and are justified, and it is with your mouth that you profess your faith and are saved.*

It's also important to remember that the same chapter which contains the most popular evangelistic verse, John 3:16, ends with both a promise and a warning, side-by-side:

> *Whoever believes in the Son has eternal life, but whoever rejects the Son will not see life, for God's wrath remains on them (John 3:36).*

As a parent, it is essential for you to get a handle on these four key truths, and the Scriptures from which they are drawn, so that you may walk your children through the gospel at any time. As you teach them God's holy standard, and discipline them toward it, the Holy Spirit will open doors for gospel conversations.[6] Perhaps it would be helpful for you as a husband or wife to practice sharing this message with your spouse so that when these opportunities arise you may be able to share the good news with your kids in a natural, not stiff, manner.

A few more tips to consider

As much as possible, use biblical language when teaching the gospel to your children. Try not to replace God's inspired Word with a clever substitute, or what you think may be easier for your kids to accept:

- Don't be afraid of using fearful words like sin, judgment, hell, or eternal punishment in conversation. Jesus used these words often. He also loved to associate with children (Luke 18:16).

- Avoid unbiblical, watered-down language about how to get saved, like, "Ask Jesus into your heart" or, "Just pray this little prayer." Scripture is infinitely more powerful than any version of the gospel you or I may create simply to stimulate a "decision for Christ" (Rom. 10:17).
- Talk about *repentance* and *faith*, which are two sides of the coin of faith. Turning to Christ for salvation is accompanied by turning away from sin and unbelief against God (Acts 20:21).
- Rather than talking about "accepting Jesus as Savior," talk about what it means to be accepted by God through Jesus the Savior, to be reconciled—no longer enemies of God, but beloved children (2 Cor. 5:18–20).
- Be patient. Remember that evangelizing your child is a lot like gardening. You

plant seeds. Then you water. Then you pray for the warmth of God's Spirit to work the soil of your child's heart. Then you plant some more. Do some weeding. And pray more. And on and on it goes. Remember that God is in charge of the harvest (1 Cor. 3:7).

Take a moment to reflect

Now this probably could remain unsaid, but I won't take that chance: You won't be able to thrill your kids with the gospel of grace if you are not thrilled with it yourself. Sometimes when we sing *Amazing Grace* at church, I am unable to sing all of the way through without tears (at least on the inside). Likewise, when we celebrate the Lord's Supper, the Holy Spirit often draws me so close to the cross of Christ that I am overwhelmed by God's grace and the depth of my Savior's love. "Jesus, keep me near the cross"[7] is a frequent prayer.

Never, never lose the wonder of God's great mercy. Be so thrilled with the gospel that your children will never be mistaken as to who you love most. If Jesus is no longer your first love, spend some time meditating on Revelation 2:1–7, and ask the Lord to rekindle the fire within you.

SIGNPOST 6

TELL THEM GOD HAS A PLAN FOR THEIR LIFE

In today's world, our kids receive mixed messages. On one hand the world tells them they are amazing, but we want them to believe God is awesome. At school they hear they're awesome, but at church they are told they're sinful (if you're part of a church that is faithful to the Bible). This leaves them confused. Therefore, what our children really need is for seemingly conflicting truths to be kept together, as a unit. This will provide them with a self-image deduced from Scripture, and prepare them to hear the gospel and respond in childlike faith. We may do this by keeping four more certainties together and applied to our kids.

God created them in a wonderful way, with a good plan

One of our family traditions is to read Psalm 139:13–16 on each of our children's birthdays. By doing so, we keep before them (and the whole family) a regular reminder of how wonderfully God has created them; they were knit together in their mother's womb by God. We want our kids to know this not so that they will think more highly of themselves, but so they will learn to praise the awesome God whose "works are wonderful." In addition, our kids need to know not only that the awesome God made them, but that He also ordained their days. God has a plan for their lives that is for their good and His glory. We need to regularly assure them of this truth.

Sin wrecked everything

After sin entered the world through Adam and Eve, the downward effects snowballed into every part of human lives. Daily we recognize the goodness of God in creation all around us, but we also see corruption in every corner of our world. Facing these realities and thinking through them biblically, rather than hiding from them or pretending they don't exist, will help guide our children to grow in discernment. Sin causes all of creation to groan for the final redemption on the future day of Christ's return (Rom. 8:22–23). Therefore, we should groan over sin too. Proverbs 8:13 says, "To fear the Lord is to hate evil; I hate pride and arrogance, evil behavior and perverse speech." When we become saddened by sin, our kids will get an idea of what the fear of the Lord looks like in daily life.

God will recreate them if they turn to Christ

The hope of the gospel is that, in Jesus, God makes sinners new. When we draw near to Jesus for salvation, we come under new ownership. We are no longer slaves to sin, but now are becoming slaves of righteousness (Rom. 6:15–18). Our kids need this hope just as much as we do! Though sin has corrupted everything in God's original, good creation, God is actively restoring sinners by His grace and renewing us to do the good works He has planned (Col. 3:10; Eph. 2:10). Let's be sure to explain this wonderful truth to our kids: "Therefore, if anyone is in Christ, the new creation has come: The old has gone, the new is here!" (2 Cor. 5:17).

God will always be with them

The same psalm describing the intricate working of God in the womb of a mother also assures us of God's omniscience and omnipresence. King David praised God for His complete knowledge of him and his ways:

You have searched me, LORD,
and you know me.
You know when I sit and when I rise;
you perceive my thoughts from afar.
You discern my going out and my lying down;
you are familiar with all my ways.
Before a word is on my tongue
you, LORD, know it completely.
(Ps. 139:1–4)

David also praised God for His constant, never-failing presence:

If I go up to the heavens, you are there;
if I make my bed in the depths, you are there.
If I rise on the wings of the dawn,
if I settle on the far side of the sea,
even there your hand will guide me,
your right hand will hold me fast.
(Ps. 139:8–10)

In light of these truths, we may confidently assure our kids of God's constant presence and conscious awareness of every detail of their life.

An appropriate "You can do it!"

Perhaps you're wondering if it's always wrong to tell your kids, "You can do it!" No, it's not. In fact, these words may be a great encouragement to them, especially when they are doubtful or discouraged. There are ways we can encourage them to be secure in the Lord without puffing up their prideful flesh. Here's just a couple of examples to get your own creative juices flowing:

- When your kindergartener falls down on her bike for the fifth time, she may begin to cry, "Mommy, I can't do it. I just can't do it." But you could say, "Sweetie, I know it's hard. But you're learning. I see how God is making you stronger every day. I know you can do it."
- When your teenage son is tempted to let a queasy stomach prevent him from sharing a personal testimony at church, he may believe "There's no way I can do this, Dad. Absolutely no way!" But you could say, "Son, I understand. I get sick to my stomach, too, every time I have to talk to a group of people. But I keep repeating to myself, 'When I am afraid, I put my trust in you' (Ps. 56:3). And I pray, 'Lord, give me the strength to do this. Help me to be a blessing to others.' How about we pray together right now? I know God is going to give you the strength to do it. Remember, you're doing this for His glory anyway."

Once we've laid the biblical groundwork for thinking rightly about themselves and God, it is appropriate for us to tell our kids, "With God's help, you can do it!"

SIGNPOST 7

TEAM UP WITH A FAITHFUL CHURCH

The old African proverb "It takes a village to raise a child" is not completely off-base. Yes, it's been used by politicians to broaden their platform for the advance of agendas, but it contains an element of truth that Christian parents should keep in mind. That is, we cannot be faithful parents without the local church. This is why, for years, I have advocated for a revised proverb: "It takes a church to raise a Christian." What do I mean?

Keep church attendance and involvement a high priority

The Bible never presents Christianity as being so personal that it becomes disconnected from the local church. We need each other! Except for sickness in the family, weekly church attendance should be expected of all children living in your house. Also, try to visit other Bible-believing churches when you are away for a weekend, or on vacation. It's such a blessing to meet others elsewhere who love Christ, and helps our kids to see that God's world is bigger than just their family and their church. Make church attendance such a habit that there's never a need for your kids to ask, "Dad, Mom, are we going to church tomorrow?" Be committed church members, not casual attenders. In his book *Set Apart: Calling a Worldly Church to a Godly Life*, Kent Hughes emphasizes the need for this commitment:

> *The entire Christian life is about commitment—first and above all to Christ, but also to the church, to family, to marriage, to friendship, to ministry. None of these will ever flourish apart from commitment.*

> *Marriage, for example, can never produce the security, satisfaction, and growth that it promises unless there is commitment. On the most elementary level, you do not have to go to church to be a Christian. You do not have to go home to be married either. But in both cases if you do not, you will have a very poor relationship. Here is the point: It is my considered belief that those who do not have the local church at the very center of their lives are likely not to make it as Christians through the opening decades of the third millennium.*[8]

To instill this commitment in our kids, we need to set the example of faithfulness to a Bible-believing, gospel-preaching church.[9]

"We *get to* go to church!"

This exclamation is frequently heard in our house. Typically, on Saturday night, I enthusiastically say to my kids, "Get your Bible and your offering. Tomorrow, we *get to* go to church!" By changing one word (from "have" to "*get*"), we completely change the atmosphere of the moment, and cultivate the anticipation of tomorrow. We also try to prime our kids to be others-focused by asking them to think of someone whom they may greet. My wife is especially good at reminding our kids to look for someone who needs a friend to talk to, especially the widows and widowers, as it teaches them to respect and value their elders.

Prepare for Sunday on Saturday night

Sunday morning worship begins on Saturday evening. Therefore, think of ways you may prepare for the Lord's Day in order that your children may grow up believing Sunday is the best day of the week. Your Sunday morning routine will also become less distracting. Practical preparations may include:

- Preparing meals. Maybe have breakfast made and the table set, or cereal boxes and bowls on the kitchen counter. Perhaps choose self-serve foods such as muffins or fruit bread, yogurt, or hard-boiled eggs. You might prepare the noon meal and set the oven before you leave for church.

- Check the car has enough gas (this was important when we lived in Missouri and had a 40-minute commute to church).
- Pick out clothes, and take care of any that need ironing.
- Find Bibles (and shoes!) and lay them out.
- Set aside your offering (2 Cor. 9:7).
- Have children take baths or showers.
- Organize anything else your children need for church (four of my children are hearing impaired, so we learnt to put fresh batteries into their hearing aids, otherwise it was not uncommon for the batteries to die at church).
- Have a worship music playlist ready to fill your house with praise.
- Get to bed early. Avoid late-night Saturday activities as much as possible, so that minds are fresh for learning.

The purpose of these suggestions is not to impose rigid rules, but simply to encourage you to do whatever will be the most helpful for your family. By limiting distraction, you may decrease tension in the home, which too often provokes Sunday morning conflicts.

Get to church early

Arriving at church 15 minutes early will not only instill in your children the vanishing trait of punctuality, but it will open the door to more opportunities for servant-like ministry. You will find there is more time to strengthen relationships, speak encouraging words, or help with the expected and unexpected tasks.

Try to avoid competitive sports on Sunday

Though Scripture gives believers liberty as to the use of the Lord's Day (Rom. 14:5), it has become increasingly important for Christian parents to carefully think through the issue of competitive sports. While I acknowledge these differences among believers as issues of conscience, my concern is that sometimes liberty becomes license, and the priority of the Lord's Day is lost. Yet Scripture makes it abundantly clear that we should not make a habit of being absent from the local church (Heb. 10:24–25). As a pastor who has been in church ministry for almost 30 years, I've talked with many parents whose children are grown. Too many now regret the low priority they placed upon church involvement. Avoiding sports teams which require Sunday involvement is one way to send the message that you, as the parent, honor the Lord *above* your child.

Take a moment to reflect

How would you describe your relationship to your church? Are you a committed member? If not, why not? If you are not a member of a church that is faithful to the Bible, and you need to know what to look for, read *Help! I Need a Church.*[10]

SIGNPOST 8

TRUST THE LORD WITH YOUR KIDS

Your child's greatest need is the one you are powerless to meet. The sooner you come to grips with this reality the better.

Sometimes parents think of salvation from sin as God throwing a life preserver to people who are drowning, but that is inadequate. Instead, we should picture ourselves and our children as already dead on the bottom of the ocean, six miles below the surface, beyond rescue by any means other than God. Salvation, as a child or an adult, is nothing short of a divine rescue mission to raise to life those who are already dead in trespasses and sin (Eph. 2:1).

Therefore, every conversion to Christ, and every life that is lived to the glory of God, is made possible by the work of the Holy Spirit. He alone has the power.

Remember, God alone saves

Too many Christian parents think of themselves as imperfect but pretty good parents who are doing their best to raise pretty good kids. (If that was your manner of thinking when you picked up this book, I hope I have shattered that notion!) The real truth is this: "Good" kids being raised in "good Christian homes" need the saving grace of God just as much as the rage-filled teenager who's responsible for a school shooting. Your child needs the intervention of the Spirit by means of the gospel just as much as the naughtiest child in your neighborhood. Stop living in a dream world. Keep this reality in mind.

Don't forget that salvation is brought about not by the will of man, but by the will of God. Nor is it inherited from one's parents, as the Gospel of John teaches:

> *Yet to all who did receive him, to those who believed in his name, he gave the right to become children of God—children born not of natural descent, nor of human decision or a husband's will, but born of God (John 1:12–13).*

Though man's will is necessarily involved in the act of believing in Christ, it is God's initiative at work. So be careful not to try to manipulate your kids into heaven. To be saved, we and our children must be born again. But we cannot do this for ourselves, or for them; each of us—as an individual—must be "born of God."

Pray for their conversion

Since the Bible unapologetically teaches "Salvation comes from the LORD" (Jon. 2:9), we should faithfully ask the Lord to do His saving work in our child's heart. Like Job, the Old Testament patriarch, we should regularly intercede for our children (Job 1:5). We should ask the Lord to do as He did for Lydia and to open the heart of our child to respond to the gospel (Acts 16:14). We should depend upon the Holy Spirit to give the breath of new life to their souls (John 3:1–8). All of this is to say let us love, train, and instruct our children diligently, as if their salvation depends upon us. But let us pray with fervent faith, knowing and resting in the reality that their salvation depends upon the grace of God.

Affirm them to the glory of God

If the Lord gives you the blessing of seeing your children come to know Jesus as Lord and Savior, commit to being an encouragement to their Christian growth. When you see little or big evidences of the Lord's work in your child's heart, be sure to affirm them. Perhaps write your kids a note on occasion, slipping it into their lunchbox, or leaving it on their dresser. In his excellent book *Practicing Affirmation*, Sam Crabtree writes of the value of verbal and written affirmation:

> *Even with the Bible's emphasis on humble self-denial and its warnings against pride, the Bible praises people—to the glory of God, ultimately. The chief end of God is not to glorify man, as humanistic thought would have it; the chief*

end of man is to glorify God by enjoying him forever. Meanwhile, the praising of people does not necessarily preclude the praising of God, if the people are commended ultimately for his glory. God is glorified in us when we affirm the work he has done and is doing in others.[11]

Generally speaking, as Christian parents, we tend to be light on commendation and heavy on criticism. Sometimes we get the strange idea that if we praise our children for their work, character, and love then they will become proud. But the apostle Paul didn't think that way. Instead, his mind's eye looked for what was praiseworthy in others. Now, mind you, he was also not afraid to give rebuke when it was necessary, as faithful parents must do. But his habit was to look for evidence of God's gracious work in the lives of others, and praise them for it (see, for example, 1 Cor. 1:4–8; Phil. 1:6–7, 25).

Take a moment to reflect

To be faithful parents we must guard against thinking too highly of ourselves or of our child's perceived goodness. We are not good parents attempting to raise good children; we are sinners saved by grace who are depending upon God, and pleading with Him, to graciously give eternal life to our children, through the gospel, by means of His grace.

It's not easy to trust the Lord with our kids, but we have the privilege to pray diligently for them while pointing them to Jesus. When we see evidence of God's grace in their attitudes and deeds, we can affirm our kids to God's glory. Proverbs 18:21 observes, "The tongue has the power of life and death." As parents, our speech may be used to build up our children, or tear them down, as we seek to model for them what it means to be a faithful follower of Jesus Christ.

Talk to the Lord about the things you've learned in this book. Confess specific ways you have failed to be faithful. Ask Him to give you wisdom and strength to shepherd your children well. At the same time, joyfully rest in Him to perform the work in your kids that only He can do.

Blessed are all who fear the LORD,
who walk in obedience to him.
You will eat the fruit of your labor;
blessings and prosperity will be yours.
Your wife will be like a fruitful vine
within your house;
your children will be like olive shoots
around your table.
Yes, this will be the blessing
for the man who fears the LORD.
(Ps. 128:1–4)

KEEP THE CONVERSATIONS GOING

Throughout this book we've been thinking about the importance of keeping God central in our parenting. We aim to do this so that, by God's grace, our kids may grow up to fear Him, know Him through Christ, and live to please the Savior more than themselves (2 Cor. 5:15). The key to this, of course, is to progressively bring the truth of God's Word to bear upon their mind and heart so that—as we pray—the Holy Spirit may reach their hearts.

It's been said that an accusation hardens the will, but a question stirs the conscience. With that in mind, here are suggested questions to stimulate spiritual conversations which may open doors to share the gospel of grace with your kids and nurture God-centered faith.

Ages 2 to 5

- What is the Bible?
- Why does Jesus say the Bible is like bread?
- Who made you?
- Why did God create you?
- What does it mean that God is awesome?
- What is sin? Where did sin come from? What does sin make you do?
- What did Jesus do on the cross? Why did God raise Him from the dead?
- What does the Bible say you *must* believe?

Ages 6 to 12

- What does it mean to fear the Lord?
- What does "awesome" mean?
- How is God awesome? What are some of His awesome works?

- What does it mean that the Bible is breathed out by God?
- How is the Bible like bread?
- What does it mean when the Bible says you are wonderfully made by God?
- What do you think God may want you to be when you grow up?
- Whose idea was it that we should be workers? How does God want you to work?
- Can you name four truths that explain God's plan of salvation?
- What is one thing you learned in your Sunday school class this week?
- What is your favorite worship song? Why?

Ages 13 to 18

- Have you ever heard someone say, "Just listen to your heart and follow wherever it leads"? How does this compare to Jeremiah 17:9? Why is this a dangerous way to think?

- How is the Bible like a personal trainer?
- What does it mean to delight in the Word of God? What habits might be present in the person who does this?
- How is the Bible like a mirror? What is one area of your heart that God's mirror is helping you see? What change does God want you to make with His help?
- What have you learned from the Bible recently?
- What does it mean that "the fear of the LORD is the beginning of wisdom" and leads to hating evil? How does this work?
- Is there a specific sin you are struggling with that you want God to take away? Do you want to talk about it?
- Name some works of God, or abilities He has given you, that make you want to shout, "God is awesome!"
- How is it possible for God to be both holy and merciful at the same time?

- Let's talk about Psalm 85:10. What does it mean that "righteousness and peace kiss each other"? How is that possible?
- What actually happened to Jesus on the cross? What happened between the Father and the Son during the crucifixion? Why?
- How does Jesus make it possible for us to be in awe of God's holiness and amazed by His love?
- Why do you think God created you to be a hard worker? How can work reflect God and be a witness for Christ?
- Can you explain to me the four truths of God's plan for salvation?
- What is one thing you learned in Sunday school (or youth group) this week?
- What is your favorite worship song? Why?

NOTES

1 R.C. Sproul, *What Does It Mean to Fear God?*, https://www.ligonier.org/blog/what-does-it-mean-fear-god/, accessed April 21, 2018.

2 Tedd Tripp, *Shepherding a Child's Heart* (Wapwallopen, PA: Shepherd Press, 1995), pp. xxi–xxii.

3 Jerry Bridges, *The Joy of Fearing God* (Colorado Springs, CO: Waterbrook Press, 2004), pp. 75.

4 Reginald Heber, "Holy, holy, holy, Lord God Almighty!" (1826).

5 John Newton, "Amazing grace, how sweet the sound" (1779).

6 My wife and I have written specifically on

this topic in a fuller, practical manner in the mini-book *Help! My Toddler Rules the House* (Shepherd Press, 2010).

7 Fanny Crosby, "Jesus, keep me near the cross" (1869).

8 R. Kent Hughes, *Set Apart: Calling a Worldly Church to a Godly Life* (Wheaton, IL: Crossway Books, 2003), pp. 136–137.

9 If you need to find a faithful church, I encourage all Americans to visit the "Church Search" feature of the 9Marks website (www.9marks.org). UK readers might like to use the search feature on The Gospel Partnerships website. (www.thegospelpartnerships.org.uk)

10 Jim Newheiser, *Help! I Need a Church* (Wapwallopen, PA: Shepherd Press, 2016).

11 Sam Crabtree, *Practicing Affirmation* (Wheaton, IL: Crossway Books, 2011), pp. 11-12.

BIBLICAL
COUNSELING
COALITION
BRINGING THE WORLD OF
BIBLICAL COUNSELING TOGETHER
PARTNER WITH US TODAY!
BiblicalCounselingCoalition.org
@biblicalcc
@BiblicalCounselingCoalition

RAISING KIDS
in a "You Can Do It!" World
Help for Parents
Paul Tautges